THE BEST
GOLFERS
OF ALL TIME

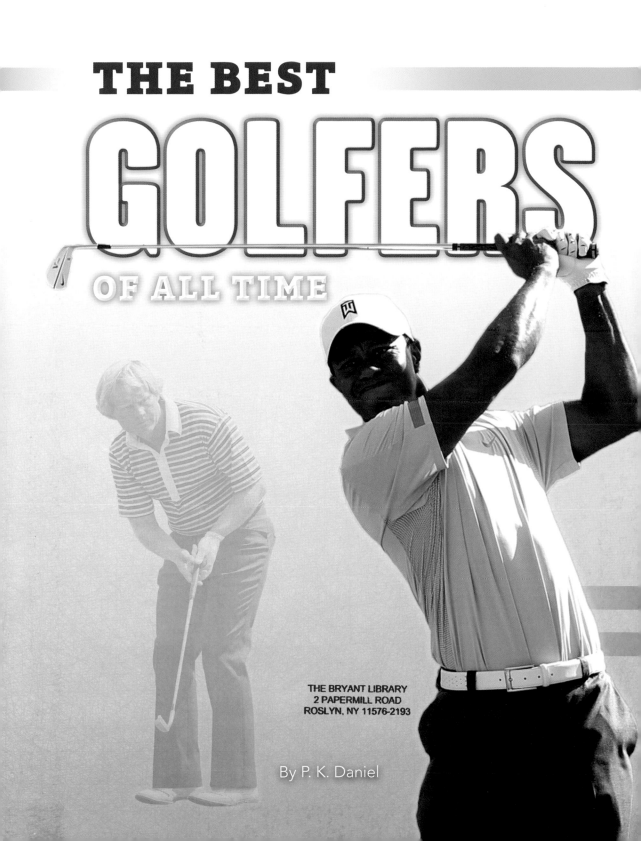

By P. K. Daniel

www.abdopublishing.com

Published by Abdo Publishing, a division of ABDO, PO Box 398166,
Minneapolis, Minnesota 55439. Copyright © 2015 by Abdo Consulting
Group, Inc. International copyrights reserved in all countries. No part
of this book may be reproduced in any form without written permission
from the publisher. SportsZone™ is a trademark and logo of Abdo
Publishing.

Printed in the United States of America, North Mankato, Minnesota
092014
012015

THIS BOOK CONTAINS
RECYCLED MATERIALS

Cover Photos: Scott Heppell/AP Images, right; AP Images, left
Interior Photos: Scott Heppell/AP Images, 1 (right); AP Images, 1 (left),
7, 9, 11, 13, 15, 19, 23, 25, 27, 31, 33, 35, 37, 39; Bettmann/Corbis,
17; Tom Sande/AP Images, 21; Ed Widdis/AP Images, 29; Rob Carr/
AP Images, 41; Phil Sandlin/AP Images, 43; Dave Martin/AP Images,
45, 47, 51; David W. Leindecker/Shutterstock Images, 49; Shutterstock
Images, 53, 59; Tony Bowler/Shutterstock Images, 55; Debby Wong/
Shutterstock Images, 57; Chris Carlson/AP Images, 61

Editor: Patrick Donnelly
Series Designer: Christa Schneider

Library of Congress Control Number: 2014944204

Cataloging-in-Publication Data
Daniel, P.K.
 The best golfers of all time / P.K. Daniel.
   p. cm. -- (Sports' best ever)
ISBN 978-1-62403-619-4 (lib. bdg.)
Includes bibliographical references and index.
1. Golf--Juvenile literature.   I. Title.
796.352--dc23

                                          2014944204

TABLE OF CONTENTS

INTRODUCTION

Golf is the ultimate game of mind and body.

The game traces its roots to Scotland in the 1400s. It has always been a physical and mental test. It takes strength and coordination to hit a golf ball to the right place. Yet mental discipline is just as important. Golfers must know the course so they can pick the best possible shot. They need creativity to recover from a tough spot in the rough. And they need nerves of steel to stand over a championship-winning putt—and make it. The ones who put it all together in the game's four major tournaments are considered legendary.

Here are some of the greatest golfers of all time.

WALTER HAGEN

In the 1920s, Walter Hagen was the biggest name in golf. He wore stylish clothes on and off the course. He loved fancy cars. He won 11 major championships. And he is believed to be the first athlete to reach $1 million in career earnings.

But life was not always a party for Hagen. He was born to a working-class family in Rochester, New York. He began caddying at age seven to help earn money for his family. When he was 12, he decided to quit school and concentrate on golf. So he went to work at the local country club. Hagen became an assistant golf pro in 1907, when he was just 15. He played in his first professional tournament in 1912. He finished eleventh.

Hagen entered the US Open in 1914 at Chicago's Midlothian Country Club. He shot an opening-round 68 and won the title with a record-tying low score of 290.

Walter Hagen, *left*, and his caddie as they prepare for the 1926 British Open.

Hagen helped form the Professional Golfers Association (PGA) of America in 1916. He went on to win the PGA Championship a record-tying five times. This included a run of four titles between 1924 and 1927. At the time, the PGA Championship was a match-play event. During Hagen's four-year title streak, he won 22 straight matches.

Hagen also had success at the British Open. He was the first US-born player to capture the British Open title. And he won it four times. In all, he collected 45 PGA Tour wins. Eleven of those wins were majors, which was still the third-most in history through 2014.

Hagen was instrumental in forming the match-play competition between the United States and Europe. Today, that competition is known as the Ryder Cup. Hagen was the captain of the first seven US teams.

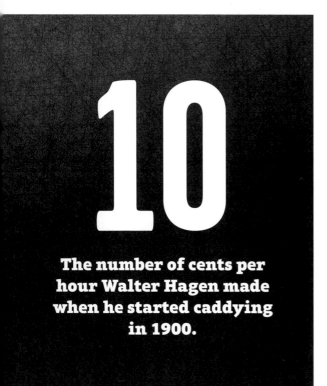

10

The number of cents per hour Walter Hagen made when he started caddying in 1900.

Walter Hagen accepts the trophy for leading the US team to victory in the 1937 Ryder Cup.

WALTER HAGEN

Hometown: Rochester, New York

Height: 5 feet 10

Birthdate: December 21, 1892

PGA Tour Victories: 45

Major Championships: 11
   US Open (1914, 1919)
   British Open (1922, 1924, 1928, 1929)
   PGA Championship (1921, 1924, 1925, 1926, 1927)

BOBBY JONES

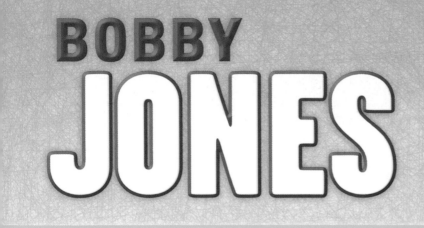

Golf is a game of etiquette. That means players are expected to have good manners. Growing up, Bobby Jones did not understand that. He had a temper. He threw his golf clubs. And when he fell short of some early expectations, he gave up.

A low point came in 1921. The 19-year-old Jones was playing the third round of the British Open. He struggled mightily on the front nine. Through 10 holes his score was already in the 50s. But instead of toughing it out, Jones did the only thing worse than posting an embarrassing final score. He picked up his ball on hole No. 11 and quit.

Jones eventually matured and learned to control his temper. He became one of the most respected golfers of all time. He never had a formal golf lesson. But he won a total of 13 major championships, all as an amateur.

Bobby Jones conquered his temper to become one of golf's first superstars.

Between 1923 and 1929, Jones won nine majors. New York City hosted a ticker-tape parade—once a traditional honor for national heroes—for him in 1926. This came after he won the US and British Opens. In 1930, Jones became the first golfer to win all four majors in one calendar year. This feat, known as the Grand Slam, earned him another ticker-tape parade in New York City.

12

The number of times Bobby Jones played in the Masters. His best finish was a tie for 13th in 1934.

Jones retired from competitive golf less than two months after winning the Grand Slam. He was only 28 years old. He went on to study engineering, English, and law at three different colleges. He eventually worked as a lawyer in his father's law firm in Georgia.

Jones also helped design the famous Augusta National Golf Club, which opened in 1933. The next year, he co-founded the Masters Tournament, which has been played at Augusta National ever since.

Bobby Jones holds his trophy for winning the 1930 British Open.

BOBBY JONES

Hometown: Atlanta, Georgia

Height: 5 feet 8

Birthdate: March 17, 1902

PGA Tour Victories: 9

Major Championships: 13
US Open (1923, 1926, 1929, 1930)
British Open (1926, 1927, 1930)
US Amateur (1924, 1925, 1927, 1928, 1930)
British Amateur (1930)

BABE DIDRIKSON ZAHARIAS

When Babe Didrikson was young, she played just about every sport she could. She was good at just about every one of them too. She was once asked if there was anything she did not play. Her reply: "Dolls."

Mildred Ella Didrikson grew up in Beaumont, Texas. She grew up playing baseball with the boys in her neighborhood. The story goes that when she started hitting home runs against them, she earned the nickname "Babe," after baseball star Babe Ruth. She later became a standout in basketball, track and field, and golf.

Didrikson entered three track-and-field events at the 1932 Olympics. She won two gold medals, setting an Olympic record in the javelin and a world record in the 80-meter hurdles. She also won a silver medal in the high jump.

Babe Didrikson was an Olympic track-and-field star before she turned her focus to golf.

After the Olympics, Didrikson concentrated on golf. Her talent and intense will to win quickly separated her from the other players. She won the first tournament she entered, in 1934. She changed her name after marrying professional wrestler George Zaharias in 1938. And she was equally dominant as Babe Didrikson Zaharias. In all, she won a total of 82 amateur and pro titles.

In 1947, Didrikson Zaharias won the Women's British Open golf tournament. She was the first American to ever win it. She even played against men in three PGA Tour events in 1945, making the cut in all of them. And she was the leading money winner on the Ladies Professional Golf Association (LPGA) tour in 1950 and 1951.

Didrikson Zaharias died of cancer in 1956 at the age of 45. The Associated Press named her the top female athlete of the first half of the twentieth century.

65

The height in inches (165 cm) of Babe Didrikson's world-record high jump at the 1932 Olympics. Judges said she jumped headfirst, so she settled for second place.

Babe Didrikson Zaharias shows off the form that made her one of the pioneers of women's golf.

BABE DIDRIKSON ZAHARIAS

Hometown: Port Arthur, Texas

Height: 5 feet 7

Birthdate: June 26, 1911

LPGA Tour Victories: 41

Major Championships: 10
  Western Open (1940, 1944, 1945, 1950)
  Titleholders Championship (1947, 1950, 1952)
  US Women's Open (1948, 1950, 1954)

Other Honors: Associated Press Female Athlete of the Year (1932, 1945–47, 1950, 1954)

BYRON NELSON

Byron Nelson was nicknamed "Lord Byron" because he was a gentleman on and off the course. He did not drink. He did not smoke. He worked hard and remained humble, even when he was the best player in the world. And although his career was short, he will always be considered royalty in the golf world.

As a young boy in Texas, Nelson mowed the greens at the local golf course. He also cleaned and fixed the members' clubs. He was caddying by age 12. He turned pro when he was 20. And five years later, he won his first major at the 1937 Masters.

A change in technology helped Nelson's career really take off. In the 1930s, golf club manufacturers began to replace their wooden shafts with steel. Nelson was one of the first players to change his swing to take advantage of the power the steel provided.

Byron Nelson signs autographs for fans in 1943.

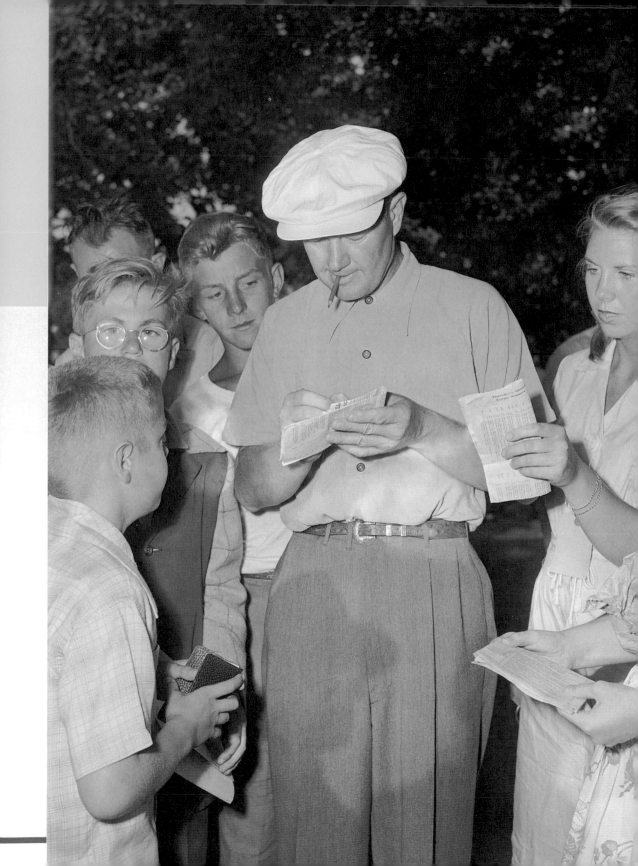

Those changes led to one of the most amazing runs in golf history.

In 1944, Nelson won eight tournaments. The next year, he won 11 straight tournaments and a total of 18 that season. No player since has come close to matching either of those records. He also had seven second-place finishes in 1945.

"Nothing prepared the world for the way he dominated his sport in 1944 and 1945," wrote Matt Schudel in the *Washington Post*.

But Nelson was not prepared for it either. The attention and pressure began to wear on him. Nelson was a simple man. He did not like being in the spotlight. So to the surprise of many, he retired from competitive golf in 1946. He was just 34. He did not leave the game entirely, though. He became a TV commentator, and he mentored young players.

113

The number of consecutive top-20 tournament finishes by Byron Nelson—a record through 2014.

Byron Nelson hits out of the rough in 1937.

BYRON NELSON

Hometown: Waxahachie, Texas

Height: 5 feet 10

Birthdate: February 4, 1912

PGA Tour Victories: 52

Major Championships: 5
Masters (1937, 1942)
US Open (1939)
PGA Championship (1940, 1945)

Other Honors: Associated Press Male Athlete of the Year (1944, 1945)

SAM SNEAD

When Sam Snead was a child, golf was a still a relatively new sport. Not many people played it, especially in the United States. There also were not nearly as many courses as there are today. But Snead was lucky. He grew up near Homestead, which is a vacation resort in Virginia. Homestead had an 18-hole golf course. And Snead quickly fell in love with the game.

Snead started gathering golf balls from the practice range when he was seven years old. By the time he was 12, he was chipping and putting into quart-sized tomato cans. He played practice rounds with his brothers, Homer and Pete. Snead also showed promise in other sports. He was a natural athlete. He starred in baseball, football, basketball, and track and field in high school.

Sam Snead lines up a putt at the first Bing Crosby Pro-Am in 1937.

In 1935, Snead entered his first golf tournament. He finished third. Two years later, Snead joined the PGA Tour. He won the second event he entered as a professional, the Oakland Open. In 1938, Snead won the Greater Greensboro Open for the first time. He went on to win it eight times. No player has ever won the same tournament that many times. Snead won his last Greater Greensboro Open in 1965. He was 52 years old. That made him the oldest man to win a tournament in PGA Tour history.

Amazingly, Snead never had a golf lesson. But Slammin' Sam won 82 PGA Tour events. Nobody had won more through 2014. He also won seven majors. The only major he did not win was the US Open, where he finished second four times.

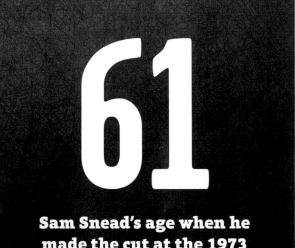

61

Sam Snead's age when he made the cut at the 1973 US Open. Through 2014, he was the oldest player to make the cut at the US Open.

US Ryder Cup captain Sam Snead, *left*, accepts the winning team's trophy in 1959.

SAM SNEAD

Hometown: Ashwood, Virginia

Height: 5 feet 11

Birthdate: May 27, 1912

PGA Tour Victories: 82

Major Championships: 7
> Masters (1949, 1952, 1954)
> British Open (1946)
> PGA Championship (1942, 1949, 1951)

Season Title: PGA Player of the Year (1949)

BEN HOGAN

Ben Hogan was at the peak of his golfing career on February 2, 1949. But on that day, a Greyhound bus hit his car head on. Hogan broke his collarbone, pelvis, and ankle in the crash. He also chipped a rib. And he suffered life-threatening blood clots.

But Hogan was not a quitter. He made a full recovery from his numerous injuries. Hogan returned to the PGA Tour in 1950 and won the US Open just 16 months after his accident. He won the PGA Player of the Year Award in 1950 and 1951. And in 1953, he won the Masters, the US Open, and the British Open. That feat came to be known as the "Hogan Slam."

Ben Hogan, *center*, with his wife, Valerie, after winning the 1950 US Open.

Hogan was born and raised in Texas. His father and grandfather owned a blacksmith business. Hogan used the skills he learned in the blacksmith shop to build golf clubs later in life. Hogan turned pro at age 17, but it took him 10 years to win his first tournament.

By then, he was ready to dominate the tour.

Hogan won the Vardon Trophy for having the lowest scoring average on the tour in 1940, 1941, and 1948. He took a two-year break from golf and enlisted in the armed forces in 1943. But through 2014, he was still fourth overall with 64 career PGA Tour wins and nine major titles.

Hogan is considered one of the best ball-strikers of all-time. And his "Hogan Slam" at age 40 is still considered one of the greatest feats in golf history.

5

The number of golfers who won all four majors in their career. Ben Hogan was the second to do it.

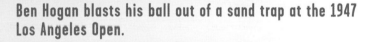

Ben Hogan blasts his ball out of a sand trap at the 1947
Los Angeles Open.

BEN HOGAN

Hometown: Stephenville, Texas

Height: 5 feet 8

Birthdate: August 13, 1912

PGA Tour Victories: 64

Major Championships: 9
    Masters (1951, 1953)
    US Open (1948, 1950, 1951, 1953)
    British Open (1953)
    PGA Championship (1946, 1948)

Season Titles: PGA Player of the Year (1948, 1950,
    1951, 1953)

Other Honors: Associated Press Male Athlete of
    the Year (1953)

ARNOLD PALMER

Arnold Palmer came from a working-class family. His dad worked at the country club in Latrobe, Pennsylvania. So the younger Palmer would hang out there as a child. That background later helped him identify with everyday fans in a sport once reserved for only the rich.

Palmer earned a golf scholarship at Wake Forest University. He won three Atlantic Coast Conference championships in college. He followed that by winning a US Amateur title in 1954. Soon after, he turned pro.

Palmer's first pro win came in 1955 at the Canadian Open. In 1958, he won the first of his four Masters championships. He was the youngest Masters winner at the time. He also finished that year first on the money list. He would match that feat three more times in the next five years.

Arnold Palmer celebrates as his putt drops to clinch his only US Open title in 1960.

Between 1960 and 1963, Palmer won 29 titles. And he became extremely popular with golf fans. His supporters became known as "Arnie's Army." They would follow him from hole to hole, cheering him on to victory. Palmer's willingness to take risky shots made his game exciting to watch.

2

The number of golfers to receive the Presidential Medal of Freedom: Jack Nicklaus and Arnold Palmer.

Palmer racked up 62 PGA Tour career wins, putting him fifth on the all-time list. He won seven major titles, missing only the PGA Championship in his bid for a career Grand Slam. He was the captain of the winning US Ryder Cup team in 1963. He also was the 1975 Ryder Cup team captain.

Palmer went on to design more than 200 courses around the world. He even popularized a famous drink. An "Arnie Palmer" is half iced tea and half lemonade. In many ways, Palmer has ensured a lasting legacy.

Jack Nicklaus, *left*, helps Arnold Palmer into his green jacket after Palmer won his fourth Masters title.

ARNOLD PALMER

Hometown: Latrobe, Pennsylvania

College: Wake Forest University

Height: 5 feet 10

Birthdate: September 10, 1929

PGA Tour Victories: 62

Major Championships: 7
Masters (1958, 1960, 1962, 1964)
US Open (1960)
British Open (1961, 1962)

Season Titles: PGA Player of the Year (1960, 1962)

MICKEY WRIGHT

Mickey Wright had lost her putting touch. After two rounds of the 1961 US Women's Open, she was tied for fourth place. She had just carded an 80 and had trouble on the greens. So that night, she practiced her putting on the carpet in her hotel room. That extra time at the Holiday Inn paid off. The next day, she stormed past the competition and won her sixth major by six strokes.

Wright took up the game at an early age. By the time she was four, she was hitting balls with her father. At age 14, she posted a round of 70. She won the United States Golf Association (USGA) Girls' Junior Championship for her first national title in 1952.

Mickey Wright is all smiles in 1961 after winning her third US Women's Open title.

Ben Hogan called Wright's swing the best he had ever seen. She is considered by many to be the greatest player in the history of the LPGA. Wright held all four majors at the same time. She won them over the 1961 and 1962 seasons. She is the only LPGA player to accomplish this. She also won 13 majors over an eight-year span. She won 10 of those majors in the 1960s, more than double the total of her nearest competitor. And she won 44 tournaments in a span of four years in the early 1960s. Through 2014, Wright ranked second all time with 82 wins.

The decorated golfer has been inducted into multiple halls of fame. *GOLF Magazine* named Wright "Golfer of the Decade" for the years 1958–1967. In 1999, the Associated Press recognized her as the top female golfer of the twentieth century.

14

The number of consecutive seasons (1956–1969) in which Wright won at least one LPGA title.

Mickey Wright lines up a putt at the 1961 US Women's Open, one day after she practiced putting in her hotel room.

MICKEY WRIGHT

Hometown: San Diego, California

College: Stanford University

Height: 5 feet 9

Birthdate: February 14, 1935

LPGA Tour Victories: 82

Major Championships: 13
    Western Open (1962, 1963, 1966)
    Titleholders Championship (1961, 1962)
    LPGA Championship (1958, 1960, 1961, 1963)
    US Women's Open (1958, 1959, 1961, 1964)

Other Honors: Associated Press Female Athlete of the Year Award (1963, 1964)

GARY PLAYER

Gary Player won his first Masters in 1961. The South African beat Arnold Palmer by one stroke. In doing so, Player became the first non-US player to win Augusta National's famed green jacket. The jacket is symbolic of winning the Masters.

Winners can borrow the jacket from the Augusta National clubhouse during the year. Player took his jacket home to South Africa, covered it in plastic, and hung it in his closet. A Masters official called Player the next year and asked him to return the jacket. Player told him he would have to come get it if Augusta wanted it back. That jacket is still in South Africa.

Growing up, Player was a standout all-around athlete. He participated in rugby, cricket, soccer, and swimming. He took up golf at age 14. Just three years later, he turned pro. And he took the golf world by storm.

Gary Player reacts after draining a birdie putt at the 1961 Masters.

Player was 29 when he became just the third man in history to win the career Grand Slam. He joined Gene Sarazen and Ben Hogan. Jack Nicklaus and Tiger Woods would also accomplish this feat. Player is the only non-American to hold that distinction through 2014.

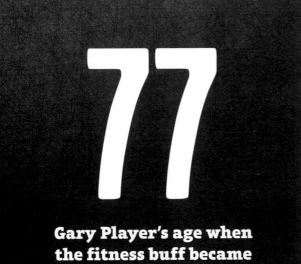

77

Gary Player's age when the fitness buff became the oldest athlete to pose for *ESPN The Magazine's* annual Body Issue.

Player left his mark on the game in many ways. He captured the career Grand Slam on the Senior Tour too, making him the only golfer to do so on both tours. He won nine majors on the PGA Tour and five more on the Senior Tour. He is also the only modern-day player to win the British Open championship in three different decades. And he is credited for spreading the popularity of golf throughout the world. Player won a total of 165 tournaments around the globe in Europe, Asia, Australia, and South Africa.

Gary Player, *right*, chats with fellow South African Trevor Immelman at the 2009 Masters.

GARY PLAYER

Hometown: Johannesburg, South Africa

Height: 5 feet 7

Birthdate: November 1, 1935

PGA Tour Victories: 24

Major Championships: 9
Masters (1961, 1974, 1978)
US Open (1965)
British Open (1959, 1968, 1974)
PGA Championship (1962, 1972)

JACK NICKLAUS

Jack Nicklaus was tied for ninth place after the first three rounds of the 1986 Masters. He entered the final round four shots off the lead. For most great golfers, overcoming a four-stroke deficit would not seem impossible. But Nicklaus was 46 years old. He had not won a PGA Tour tournament in two years. Many fans thought he was washed up.

Nicklaus proved them wrong that day. He played the first eight holes in even par. It was hard to believe what happened next. Nicklaus sunk birdies at holes 9, 10, and 11. The tide had started to turn. Nicklaus took the lead when he sunk a twisting 11-foot birdie putt on the 17th hole. He finished the day with a final-round 65 to win that Masters by one stroke. And he became the oldest player ever to win the green jacket.

Jack Nicklaus watches his birdie putt drop on the 17th green during the final round of the 1986 Masters.

Nicklaus had already cemented himself as perhaps the greatest golfer in history. That Masters championship simply put an exclamation point on his amazing career. Nicklaus won a record 18 majors. He won all four majors at least three times. His 73 PGA Tour wins rank him third all time through 2014. He also won two US Amateur titles.

Nicklaus was nicknamed "the Golden Bear" for his solid frame and blond hair. He started playing golf as a 10-year-old growing up in Ohio. He was just 13 when he became the youngest person to qualify for that year's US Junior Amateur. He also ran track and field and played football, baseball, and basketball as a child. Nicklaus now helps other kids play golf through a program called The First Tee.

2

The number of golfers who have won each of the four majors three times—Tiger Woods and Jack Nicklaus.

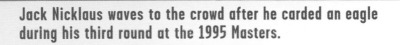

Jack Nicklaus waves to the crowd after he carded an eagle during his third round at the 1995 Masters.

JACK NICKLAUS

Hometown: Columbus, Ohio

College: Ohio State University

Height: 5 feet 10

Birthdate: January 21, 1940

PGA Tour Victories: 73

Major Championships: 18
Masters (1963, 1965, 1966, 1972, 1975, 1986)
US Open (1962, 1967, 1972, 1980)
British Open (1966, 1970, 1978)
PGA Championship (1963, 1971, 1973, 1975, 1980)

Season Titles: PGA Player of the Year (1967, 1972, 1973, 1975, 1976)

PHIL
MICKELSON

Going into the 2004 Masters, Phil Mickelson had won 22 PGA tournaments. But he had never won a major. He had finished in second or third place eight times. Fans began to wonder if he would ever break through to win a major.

Mickelson answered those questions in dramatic fashion at Augusta National. Mickelson spent most of the fourth round chasing leader Ernie Els. He finally caught Els with a birdie on the 16th hole. Then he won his first major with another birdie on the final hole of the tournament. Mickelson closed the day with five birdies in the final seven holes to win the green jacket. He had finally shed the title of the best golfer who had never won a major.

Phil Mickelson celebrates after winning his first major, the 2004 Masters.

Mickelson took an early interest in golf. As a toddler, he mimicked his father's right-handed swing. He actually mirrored his dad, which is why the natural right-hander learned to play golf left-handed. "Lefty" earned a full scholarship to Arizona State University. He won three national college titles there. In 1990, he became the only left-handed player to win the US Amateur.

Mickelson followed that by winning his first PGA Tour tournament in January 1991. He was still an amateur when he won the Northern Telecom Open in Tucson, Arizona. He turned professional at age 22. Through 2014, Mickelson had 42 PGA Tour wins, including five major championships. He had been a runner-up at the US Open six times. Many golf observers, including Jack Nicklaus, have called Mickelson one of the greatest players ever.

3

The number of consecutive years (1990–92) Phil Mickelson won the Haskins Award, which is given to the best college golfer in the United States.

Phil Mickelson hits a shot at the 2009 US Open.

PHIL MICKELSON

Hometown: San Diego, California

College: Arizona State University

Height: 6 feet 3

Birthdate: June 16, 1970

PGA Tour Victories: 42*

Major Championships: 5*
Masters (2004, 2006, 2010)
British Open (2013)
PGA Championship (2005)
*Through 2014

ANNIKA SORENSTAM

Annika Sorenstam is one of the most decorated golfers in the women's game. But that was not enough to stoke her competitive fire. The Swedish star made her biggest headlines in 2003 when she competed against men in a PGA Tour event.

Sorenstam missed the cut at the Bank of America Colonial, but that was not the point. She was the first woman in 58 years to play in a men's tournament. And she held her own. In fact, she tied for first in driving accuracy. Some people criticized Sorenstam for competing against the men. They thought it was a publicity stunt. But she was an inspiration to others, including young female players.

Annika Sorenstam escapes a sand trap at the 2003 Colonial.

Brittany Lincicome, for example, has won five LPGA tournaments through 2014. She was 16 years old when she watched Sorenstam play Colonial. "I remember thinking how really cool it was," Lincicome said. "I idolized Annika, and she was inspiring to watch. To have the courage to compete against the men spoke volumes about what a great athlete she was."

Sorenstam played professionally for 15 years. During that time, no one was better in women's golf. She won 72 LPGA events, 17 international events, and 10 majors. Her $22 million in career earnings is a record. Plus she won eight Rolex Player of the Year Awards and six Vare Trophies. The trophy is given to the golfer with the lowest scoring average each year. Sorenstam was at the peak of her game from 2003 to 2005. The Associated Press named her the Female Athlete of the Year all three of those years.

59

Annika Sorenstam's score in the second round of the 2001 Standard Register Ping. She was the only woman to break 60 in competitive play through 2014.

Annika Sorenstam was an eight-time winner of the Rolex Player of the Year Award.

ANNIKA SORENSTAM

Hometown: Bro, Sweden

College: University of Arizona

Height: 5 feet 6

Birthdate: October 9, 1970

LPGA Tour Victories: 72

Major Championships: 10
Kraft Nabisco Championship (2001, 2002, 2005)
LPGA Championship (2003–05)
US Women's Open (1995, 1996, 2006)
Women's British Open (2003)

Season Titles: LPGA Tour Player of the Year (1995, 1997, 1998, 2001–05)

TIGER
WOODS

Businesses often give endorsement deals to athletes who they think will make it big. Nike projected Tiger Woods would do just that. The sports apparel company signed him to a record five-year, $40 million contract when Woods was just 19.

Nike was impressed with Woods's phenomenal amateur career. He had become the youngest winner of the US Junior Amateur Championship at 15. He had also won three straight US Junior titles (1991–93).

Woods turned professional in 1996. He quickly began winning tournaments and racking up major titles. In 1996, Woods was named *Sports Illustrated*'s Sportsman of the Year. He won his first major, the 1997 Masters, by a record 12 shots. Soon, he became the top-ranked player in the world.

Tiger Woods tees off wearing his trademark red shirt in the fourth round of the Emirates Australian Open in 2011.

The golf world was fascinated with Woods. He sparked a boom in the game's popularity around the world. People could not get enough of "Tigermania." If Woods was in contention, TV ratings soared. Seeing him prowl the course in his trademark red shirt became a Sunday tradition. Courses began to lengthen many of their holes to "Tiger-proof" them because he hit his drives so far. By 2008, Woods trailed only Jack Nicklaus in major titles. He was third in wins. And he was being projected as the greatest golfer of all time. It appeared nothing could hold him back.

But then his career hit a big snag. Marital problems and multiple injuries sidetracked him beginning in 2009. Through 2014, he had gone six years without winning a major. Whether or not Woods recaptures his glory days, his impact on the game remains historic.

6

The number of consecutive tournaments Tiger Woods won in 2000. It was the first time in 48 years that anybody had won that many in a row.

Tiger Woods changed golf with his tremendous distance off the tee.

TIGER WOODS

Hometown: Cypress, California

College: Stanford University

Height: 6 feet 1

Birthdate: December 30, 1975

PGA Tour Victories: 79*

Major Championships: 14*
    Masters (1997, 2001, 2002, 2005)
    US Open (2000, 2002, 2008)
    British Open (2000, 2005, 2006)
    PGA Championship (1999, 2000, 2006, 2007)

Season Titles: PGA Player of the Year (1997, 1999–2003, 2005–07, 2009, 2013)
*Through 2014

INBEE PARK

Inbee Park's favorite number is one.
"That is what I want to be and where I wish to stay," she said.

Park achieved the number one ranking in the world through hard work, dedication, and a lot of talent. She held the top spot in the Rolex world golf rankings for 59 weeks between April 15, 2013, and June 1, 2014. By that time in her career, she had won nine LPGA titles, including four majors. And she was just 25 years old.

With encouragement from her dad, Park started playing golf when she was 10 years old. She moved from her home in South Korea to the United States at age 12. Her dream was to play on the LPGA Tour. And after a strong junior career, she turned pro at age 18.

Inbee Park took over the top spot in the women's world golf rankings in 2013.

In 2013, Park became the first player in the modern era to win the first three major championships of a season. The only other player to do that on the LPGA Tour was Babe Didrikson Zaharias in 1950, when there were only three majors. Park won the Kraft Nabisco Championship, the Wegmans LPGA Championship, and the US Women's Open. After winning the Kraft Nabisco Championship, she took the traditional winner's plunge into Poppie's Pond. She called it her best on-course memory.

In an era featuring many outstanding players from South Korea, Park has risen above the pack. She topped the tour's earnings list in 2012 and 2013. In 2013, she also won the Rolex Player of the Year Award. She was the first South Korean in LPGA history to win the award.

70.21

Inbee Park's scoring average in 2012. That earned Park her first Vare Trophy.

Inbee Park and her caddie celebrate in Poppie's Pond after Park won the 2013 LPGA Championship.

INBEE PARK

Hometown: Seoul, South Korea

College: Kwangwoon University

Height: 5 feet 6

Birthdate: July 12, 1988

LPGA Tour Victories: 11*

Major Championships: 5*
    Kraft Nabisco Championship (2013)
    LPGA Championship (2013, 2014)
    US Women's Open (2008, 2013)

Season Titles: LPGA Player of the Year (2013)
*Through 2014

HONORABLE MENTIONS

Patty Berg – One the pioneers of women's golf and the first president of the LPGA, Berg won 60 tournaments and a record 15 majors between 1941 and 1958.

Billy Casper – Casper won at least one PGA Tour event for 16 straight seasons (1956–71).

Nancy Lopez – Named "Golfer of the Decade" by *GOLF Magazine* for the years 1978–87, Lopez won 48 LPGA Tour events, including three major championships.

Gene Sarazen – Sarazen was the first golfer to complete the career Grand Slam and was credited with inventing the modern sand wedge.

Louise Suggs – Another pioneer in women's golf, Suggs was recognized by the LPGA as one of its top 50 players and teachers. She collected 61 tournament wins to rank fourth all time on the LPGA list and was inducted into the World Golf Hall of Fame.

Harry Vardon – One of golf's first superstars, Vardon won a record six British Open championships between 1896 and 1914, a record that still stood in 2014.

Tom Watson – The PGA Player of the Year six times and the leading money winner on the tour five times, Watson won eight majors among his 39 career victories.

Karrie Webb – One of the LPGA's dominant players in the 1990s and 2000s, Webb won six major titles and became the first player in LPGA history to achieve the Super Career Grand Slam, winning all five majors played during her career.

Kathy Whitworth – The LPGA Tour Player of the Year seven times in an eight-year span (1966–69, 1971–73), Whitworth won 88 LPGA Tour titles, more than any other golfer on either the LPGA or PGA Tours.

GLOSSARY

amateur
An athlete who competes without being paid.

birdie
A score of one-under par on a hole.

cut
Usually the halfway point of a tournament. Players who make the cut by posting the best scores advance to the final rounds.

grand slam
Winning all four of the major championships in a calendar year.

major championships
Also known as majors, they are the four biggest tournaments on the PGA and LPGA Tours.

match play
A scoring system that pits two golfers head-to-head, with the winner determined by which player wins the most holes.

par
The score a good player is expected to make on a hole—a three, four, or five, depending on the hole's difficulty.

rough
Tall or thick grass on a golf course that can trap a player's ball.

FOR MORE INFORMATION

Further Readings

Hogan, Ben and Herbert Warren Wind. *Five Lessons: The Modern Fundamentals of Golf*. Trumbull, CT: NYT Special Services, 1985.

Howell, Brian. *Golf*. Minneapolis, MN: Abdo Publishing, 2012.

Howell, Brian. *The Masters*. Minneapolis, MN: Abdo Publishing, 2013.

Websites

To learn more about Sports' Best Ever, visit **booklinks.abdopublishing.com**. These links are routinely monitored and updated to provide the most current information available.

INDEX

ABOUT THE AUTHOR

P. K. Daniel is an editor, reporter, and writer. She spent 15 years at the *San Diego Union-Tribune*, where she was recognized with a Special Merit award for editing, a U-Team award for collaboration, and several headline-writing honors. Her work has appeared in *Baseball America*, *SB Nation Longform*, TeamUSA.org, *U-T San Diego*, *Washington Post*, *Lower Extremity Review*, and *Sport Magazine*.